Would You Rather?

Thanksgiving Edition

With Fun
Illustrations

**Funny Scenarios, Wacky
Choices and Hilarious Situations
For Kids and Family**

RIDDLELAND

Table of Contents

Bonus Book!

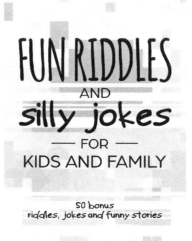

FUN RIDDLES
AND
silly jokes
— FOR —
KIDS AND FAMILY

50 bonus
riddles, jokes and funny stories

RIDDLELAND

https://pixelfy.me/riddlelandbonus

Thank you for buying this book. We would like to share a special bonus as a token of appreciation. It is a collection of 50 original jokes, riddles, and two super funny stories!

Introduction

"Gratitude unlocks the fullness of life.
It turns what we have into enough."
~ **Melody Beattle**

We would like to personally thank you for purchasing this book. ***Would You Rather? Thanksgiving Edition*** is a collection of the funniest scenarios, wacky choices, and hilarious situations for kids and adults to choose from.

These questions are an excellent way to get a conversation started in a fun and exciting way. Also, by asking "Why?" after a "Would you rather" question, you may find interesting answers and learn a lot about a person.

We wrote this book because we want children to be encouraged to read more, think, and grow. As parents, we know that when children play games and learn, they are being educated while having so much fun that they don't even realize they're learning and developing valuable life skills. 'Would you Rather …' is one of our favorite games to play as a family. Some of the 'would you rather …' scenarios have had us in fits of giggles, others have generated reactions such as: "Eeeeeeuuugh, that's gross!" and yet others still really make us think and reflect and consider our decisions.

Besides having fun, playing the game also has other benefits such as:

- **Communication** – This game helps children to interact, read aloud, and listen to others. It's a great way to connect. It's a fun way for parents to get their children interacting with them without a formal, awkward conversation. The game can also help to get to know someone better and learn about their likes, dislikes, and values.

- **Builds Confidence** - Children get used to pronouncing vocabulary, asking questions and it helps to deal with shyness.

- **Develops Critical Thinking** – It helps children to defend and justify the rationale for their choices and can generate discussions and debates. Parents playing this game with young children can give them prompting questions about their answers to help them reach logical and sensible decisions.

- **Improves Vocabulary** – Children will be introduced to new words in the questions, and the context of them will help them remember them because the game is fun.

- **Encourages Equality and Diversity** – Considering other people's answers, even if they differ from your own, is important for respect, equality, diversity, tolerance, acceptance, and inclusivity. Some questions may get children to think about options available to them, that don't fall into gendered stereotypes, i.e., careers or activities that challenge the norm.

The Laugh Challenge
Would you Rather?
Thanksgiving Edition

How do you play?

At least two players are needed to play this game. Face your opponent and decide who is **Turkey 1** and **Turkey 2**. If you have 3 or 4 players, you can decide which players belong to **Turkey Group 1** and **Turkey Group 2**. The goal of the game is to score points by making the other players laugh. The first player to a score of 10 points is the **Round Champion**.

What are the rules?

Turkey 1 starts first. Read the questions aloud and choose an answer. The same player will then explain why they chose the answer in the silliest and wackiest way possible. If the reason makes the Turkey 2 laugh, then Turkey 1 scores a funny point. Take turns going back and forth and write down the score.

How do you get started?

Flip a coin. The Turkey that guesses it correctly starts first.

Bonus Tip: Making funny voices, silly dance moves or wacky facial expression will make your opponent laugh!

Most Importantly:
Remember to have fun and enjoy the game!

Eat a turkey that is still raw OR eat a
pumpkin pie with a soggy crust and runny
filling that is not fully baked?

Eat the entire Thanksgiving dinner using only
your hands, including the cranberries, OR eat
the entire dinner without using your hands?

Would You Rather...

Have a snowball fight using sticky clumps of mashed potatoes OR have a water fight using cranberry sauce?

Have your lawn chair break in half while you're sitting on it around the bonfire OR have a black crow fly by and poop on your head?

Eat Thanksgiving dinner out of your dog's food bowl OR only be able to eat the scraps and crumbs that your family drops onto the floor during the meal?

Eat your mashed potatoes topped with a cranberry flavored gravy OR eat a bowl of stuffing that has tons of liver and onions?

Would you Rather...

Eat Thanksgiving dinner surrounded by snow and ice in Antarctica OR surrounded by palm trees on a tropical island?

Spill a cup of hot chocolate all over your shoes so they squish whenever you take a step OR have scratchy straw in your socks so it keeps scraping your ankles whenever you take a step?

Would You Rather...

Accidentally drop and break one of your mom's special china plates OR accidentally break your drinking glass and get a piece of it stuck in your finger when you try to clean it up?

Eat Thanksgiving dinner with only your teacher and classmates at school OR only with your family at home, no guests allowed?

Would you Rather...

Be in charge of cooking the entire Thanksgiving meal by yourself OR do everyone's dinner dishes all by yourself?

Rake and gather up twenty big bags of fallen leaves for $5 OR pay a friend $10 to rake up the twenty big bags of fallen leaves?

Have the flu on Thanksgiving and miss getting to eat dinner with the family OR have the flu on Christmas and miss getting to open your presents with the family?

Eat Thanksgiving dinner served up by your school's cafeteria lunch ladies OR outside on a giant picnic table on a breezy day?

Would You Rather...

Wear just a tablecloth to Thanksgiving dinner with your family OR a fancy outfit that is two sizes too tight?

Find a piece of pumpkin shell baked into your pumpkin pie OR eat a spoonful of really really lumpy mashed potatoes?

Peel potatoes using only your teeth OR eat turkey that has already been chewed up by someone else?

Be able to use your mashed potatoes in place of your school glue bottle OR paint a masterpiece using only a bowl of cooked cranberries?

Have teeth that are the color of turkey gravy OR eyes that are the color of cranberries?

Eat a bowl of tart cranberries that have no added sugar and taste like lemons OR eat a whole bowl of mashed turnips buried in a pool of gravy?

Eat just meat (meaning only turkey) OR eat only vegetables (mashed potatoes, yams, green bean casserole) for Thanksgiving dinner?

Catch the winning football game touchdown, but get tackled in the end zone and barf up your dinner OR drop the ball instead of scoring the winning touchdown and have everyone ignore you for the rest of the day?

Get super wrinkly fingers from doing the family's Thanksgiving dishes OR burn your fingers helping your dad carve the Thanksgiving turkey?

Sit next to your uncle who always unbuttons his pants halfway through the meal OR next to your little brother or sister who always burps loudly during the meal?

Would you Rather...

Scoop all your Thanksgiving food onto your plate using only your hands OR mash the potatoes by stepping on them with your bare feet?

Spend your afternoon pulling little turkey bits off the turkey OR spend your morning peeling potatoes to make mashed potatoes?

Eat sweet potatoes made by your grandma that are just white potatoes with a bunch of sugar OR eat rolls made by your mom that are super hard and crusty and coated in butter?

Have to eat the scraps of food off someone else's plate OR have to switch silverware with someone else after they've started eating?

Would you Rather...

Choke on a piece of turkey during dinner and end up spitting half-chewed turkey all over everyone's food OR have to eat everything on your plate after your grandma sneezes all over your food?

Fish your grandma's pair of fake teeth out of her glass of apple juice OR go into the bathroom after your grandpa used it and didn't turn on the fan?

Would you Rather...

Accidentally pass gas loudly while your family is giving thanks before the meal OR snort apple juice out of your nose when your dad tells a funny joke during the meal?

Use pumpkin pie scented shampoo and conditioner OR wash your hair using a can of pumpkin pie filling?

Get caught passing green beans under the table to your dog OR get caught kicking your little brother or sister under the table?

Sleep all night with a bare tree branch tapping on your window OR with a chipper owl "hoo'ing" through the night right outside your window?

Would you Rather...

Dress up in a giant turkey costume that makes you super sweaty OR have real turkey feathers glued all over your body?

Go on a hayride with a really gassy and smelly horse pulling you OR go on a hayride sitting next to someone who babbles nonstop the entire time?

Would you Rather...

Have a pet fish cracker called Cranberry floating in a fishbowl next to your bed OR a pet potato called Spud you drag on a leash everywhere you go?

Make a snow fort out of a giant pile of mashed potatoes OR dig a snow tunnel through a big stack of mashed yams?

Would you Rather...

Have everyone say one thing they're grateful for all at the same time before the meal OR have to go one by one and say something you're grateful for before you can eat?

Climb a tree and jump off it into a giant pile of dry crunchy leaves OR onto a bunch of stacked square hay bales?

Eat Thanksgiving dinner restaurant style with you being the waiter or waitress OR buffet style where everyone lines up to serve their own food - starting with oldest to youngest?

Have a new rule that kids eat last at Thanksgiving OR kids eat first but only get to eat the food that their parents put on their plates?

Would you Rather...

Grow a pig's tail and a snout if you eat a second helping at Thanksgiving dinner OR have your stomach blow up like a big balloon if you eat a second helping?

Eat a giant bowl of yucky orange pumpkin soup OR drink a cranberry green bean casserole smoothie?

Would you Rather...

Switch plates of food with your grandpa OR your younger brother or sister?

Hold hands with someone's hot and sweaty hand while giving thanks OR have someone hold your hand so tightly that it goes numb?

Make a sandcastle out of goopy mashed potatoes OR eat a mashed potato sandcastle sculpted by your little brother or sister's dirty hands?

Eat a pumpkin pie made from sweet potatoes OR a Thanksgiving chicken instead of a turkey?

Eat so much that you pass out during dinner and your face lands in a plateful of mashed yams OR in a giant gravy bowl?

Look around the table and see that everyone has at least one piece of food stuck to their face that they don't know about OR have a piece of food stuck to your face that you don't know about and no one tells you about?

Would you Rather...

Be so hungry at dinner time that you stuff a whole bunch of steaming hot food in your face and badly burn your mouth OR have to wait so long for everyone to give thanks before eating that your food is ice cold by the time you get to eat?

Bob for apples in a giant tub of jellied cranberries OR in a giant tub of buttery mashed yams?

Would you Rather...

Sit in a chair that is made for someone much smaller than you so you look huge on a tiny chair OR have to share a chair with your brother or sister because you ran out of chairs to go around the table?

Lick your dad's plate clean after eating dinner OR eat your dinner off a plate licked clean by your dog?

Eat pumpkin pie baked in a raw pumpkin shell OR eat a pumpkin pie topped with whipped mashed potatoes instead of whipped cream?

Eat a bag of potato chips instead of mashed potatoes and gravy OR a package of beef jerky instead of Thanksgiving turkey?

Eat a pound of creamy yellow butter OR drink a gallon of thick brown gravy?

Wake up at 5am to put the turkey in the oven on Thanksgiving OR oversleep you and no one wakes you up in time to eat turkey dinner with the family?

Would you Rather...

Eat black and burned turkey for Thanksgiving OR have no turkey to eat on Thanksgiving?

Weave Thanksgiving dinner placemats for everyone out of dried corn husks OR gather 1,000 acorns to make a massive wreath for your front door?

Would You Rather...

Try to eat your dinner with swim flippers on your hands OR try to sip your drink with a duck's bill instead of a mouth?

Celebrate Thanksgiving by complaining about stuff all day long instead of giving thanks OR eat Thanksgiving dinner at a table where no one can talk?

Would you Rather...

Have to babysit your younger siblings and cousins while the rest of the family plays games OR get stuck listening to your half-deaf grandparent yell stories at you about their childhood?

Lick the person's fingers who sits next to you at dinner OR have the person who sits next to you lick your fingers?

Would you Rather...

Eat Thanksgiving dinner standing at the table OR sitting with your legs crossed on the floor because you don't have a chair?

Eat lima bean casserole because you're out of green beans OR pumpkin pie made from squash because the store had sold out of canned pumpkin?

Take a bath in a big tub of melted butter OR
use a stick of butter to wash yourself instead
of a bar of soap?

Go swimming in an outdoor pool on a crisp cool
fall day and get covered in goosebumps OR be
a kite that another kid is flying on a really
windy day?

Be like Goldilocks and eat food that is way too hot OR way too cold at Thanksgiving dinner?

Eat your entire Thanksgiving dinner blended into a smoothie OR only be able to eat one kind of food all day on Thanksgiving Day?

Have your hair smell like stuffing made with chicken liver OR your feet smell like turkey gravy for a week?

Be able to squirt sticky caramel out of your belly button OR have the head of a sunflower that is filled with yummy sunflower seeds you can eat?

Run a Turkey Trot race (3.1 miles) dressed in a turkey ballerina tutu OR run a Turkey Trot race right after eating Thanksgiving dinner?

BURRRP!

Ask and answer gross "Would You Rather" questions with your family over dinner OR hear the same old family stories you hear every year while you eat dinner?

Would you Rather...

Have your cat jump up onto the table during dinner and run on top of all of the food OR have your dog pull down the tablecloth and everything from the table onto the floor during dinner?

Drink a glass of boiled potato juices OR eat cooked sweet potato skins?

Would You Rather...

Spend three hours Thanksgiving grocery shopping with your mom OR write a list of one hundred things you are grateful for as a school project?

Eat sweet potatoes with a bunch of really hard marshmallows in them OR mashed sweet potatoes that still have the skin on?

Have green beans from the casserole for eyebrows OR slimy cranberries for eyeballs?

Have a cafeteria meal turkey dinner with lunch meat turkey sandwich slices instead of big juicy pieces of turkey OR find out that the mashed potatoes they are serving are powdered flakes of potato with water added to them?

Eat Thanksgiving dinner out of take-out foam containers OR using your little sister's doll-sized china tea set?

Get pumpkin pie crust crumbs all over the keyboard of your computer OR mashed potatoes and gravy smeared all over the computer screen?

Bake the apple pie and forget to add sugar to it so there are just really sour apples baked into a crust OR accidentally leave the vanilla ice cream on the counter so it is poured on top of your pie like gravy?

Eat a completely meat free Thanksgiving dinner OR eat a Thanksgiving dinner that has meat in everything?

Sit next to your bearded uncle at Thanksgiving and eat all of the crumbs that fall onto your plate off his beard OR sit next to your aunt who keeps pinching and squeezing your cheeks all through the meal?

Build with Legos a cabin in the woods that you can live in OR a boat that you can sail on the lake in?

Pour butter over everything you eat for Thanksgiving OR eat your entire meal without using butter?

Eat a big stack of smoky turkey-flavored pancakes covered with gravy OR a juicy pumpkin pie-flavored hamburger topped with whipped cream?

Show up to Thanksgiving dinner dressed as Santa Claus, complete with a big white fuzzy beard OR as a plumped-up turkey, with giant tail feathers sticking out of your rear end?

Jump in a bouncy house made from roasted marshmallows OR drive bumper cars in a rink made of jellied cranberries?

Would you Rather...

Only be able to eat foods that you have made for Thanksgiving dinner OR only be able to eat food that matches the color of the outfit you are wearing to dinner?

Spill dark red cranberries all over your pants OR sit in a pool of gravy that was spilled on your chair?

Sit on a chair that has food smeared all over it OR eat your meal off a dirty plate and with a dirty fork?

Scrape dried mashed potatoes and gravy from the bottom of school cafeteria tables OR pick up squished green beans one by one with your fingers from the cafeteria floor?

Would you Rather...

Smuggle Thanksgiving leftovers into your pockets for later OR smuggle leftovers into your socks for later?

Find a plate of week old Thanksgiving leftovers that you forgot about under your bed OR find a big crusty blob of dried mashed potatoes in your belly button when you go to put on your pjs?

Captain a sailboat in an ocean of brown gravy
OR hike up a mountain of mashed potatoes?

Eat Thanksgiving dinner on a table that is
really sticky so everything that touches it
sticks to the table OR on a table that is
really slippery so the dishes and silverware
keep sliding right off of the table?

Go to school like the Pilgrims, and not be able to use pens, markers, and glue sticks OR not be able to use computers?

Spend six hours driving to your family's Thanksgiving celebration OR spend six days preparing food for your family's Thanksgiving celebration?

Cook your entire Thanksgiving dinner outside over a fire like the Pilgrims might have done OR only be able to eat food for Thanksgiving that can be cooked in a microwave?

Have to sit on a chair seat made from sticky marshmallow fluff OR sit on a seat made from lumpy pecan pie?

Would You Rather...

Have your grandpa fall asleep on your shoulder while watching the after-dinner football game OR have to do the dishes with your grandma while she tells you all about knitting?

Eat extra crunchy roasted turkey-flavored potato chips OR drink super fizzy cranberry-flavored soda?

Drizzle everything you eat with cinnamon caramel sauce OR find pieces of hay in everything you eat for the whole month of October?

Play a game of backyard football using a buttered dinner roll OR watch your favorite professional football team play a game using a buttered dinner roll?

Have a scarecrow's itchy stiff straw for hair OR be stuck on a pole in the middle of a cornfield like a real scarecrow for a day?

Sleep in a bed of musty smelling crunchy leaves OR sleep curled up on top of a hay bale that makes you sneeze over and over?

Would you Rather...

Use a pumpkin pie flavored toothpaste for one week OR eat an entire package of pumpkin pie flavored bubble gum in one day?

Go through a corn maze on a really dark night and have your flashlight batteries die OR keep running into the same annoying and loud group of kids while going through the maze?

Would you Rather...

Be followed the whole way to school by a pack of curiously fluffy squirrels OR try to eat a bowl full of acorns for lunch?

Hear the sound of crunchy leaves everywhere you walk OR hear the sound of a really windy day in your ears all of the time?

Dip your head into a bowl of melted caramel OR create a school art sculpture using melted caramel?

WOW! THAT'S SWEET!

Eat a peanut butter and jelly sandwich made with pumpkin bread OR eat an apple butter and jelly sandwich on regular sandwich bread?

Have really bad fall allergies that make you sneeze five times every minute OR get hiccups five times a day?

Be a fall tree that has really ugly colored wilted leaves OR be a fall tree that drops all of its leaves in one day and is naked the rest of fall?

Spend a fall afternoon chopping logs wearing a red and black checkered shirt like a lumberjack OR spend your fall afternoon dragging the heavy logs that a lumberjack chopped across a field to build a log cabin?

Play hide and seek in a hay bale maze OR go bowling using pumpkins instead of bowling balls?

Would you Rather...

Have a scarecrow at your front door who seems to follow you with his eyes whenever you go in your house OR a shifty scarecrow that mysteriously rides your school bus and always has a seat to himself?

Have everything you eat in autumn taste like sweet squashy fresh pumpkin OR super sugary candy corns?

Accidentally wear your big pink bunny slippers instead of your sneakers to school OR on pajama day find a big hole in the back of your pajamas that shows your underwear?

Finger paint with ruby red cranberries OR stringy raw orange pumpkin guts?

Have your head turn into a big orange pumpkin with leafy vines for hair OR a big red shiny apple with worm holes for eyes?

Wear a sweater that your cat unravels by pulling on a loose thread OR knit a sweater as a gift for your mom that turns out to have one sleeve MUCH shorter than the other?

Scoop out a pumpkin for carving with your tongue OR wear the expression of your Jack O'Lantern on your face for a week?

Go to an outdoor movie about crazy squirrels in a park full of squirrels OR watch an outdoor movie about crazy black crows in the middle of a cornfield with a bunch of black crows?

Eat a whole pumpkin pie that is covered in ketchup OR eat a whole apple pie that is covered in mustard?

Find leftover food scraps in the cafeteria and store them in a tree for later like a squirrel would OR spend your days climbing up and down trees and hopping across fences like a squirrel?

Stand under a tree for an hour with apples that are constantly hitting you on the head OR make applesauce by squishing apples in a tub with your toes?

Fall off the back of a hayride trailer while on a ride with your classmates OR get your foot run over by the hayride trailer while you're trying to get on it?

Have a giant pumpkin to sit on instead of a desk chair OR have an all-day gym class at a pumpkin patch where you have to roll giant pumpkins around the patch?

Eat a bowl of apple cinnamon oatmeal made from rotten apples OR drink a glass of apple juice made from rotten apples?

Spend a week sitting in a bird's nest high up in a tree OR spend a week dodging a bird that keeps dive bombing you every time you step outside?

Have a food fight in the cafeteria with mashed potatoes and gravy OR creamy chocolate pudding?

Make a scarecrow out of straw on a windy day OR try to rake up all the fallen leaves in your yard on a windy day?

Play on a playground where there are wasps buzzing everywhere OR on a playground that is totally buried in crusty leaves?

Be made of straw so you can never get hurt when you play dodgeball in gym class OR have a squirrel's tail that you can use to play kickball in gym class?

Sit in a classroom all day that smells really strongly of pumpkin spice OR sit in a classroom all day that smells really strongly of moldy leaves?

Would you Rather...

Spend all day climbing ladders to pick apples at an apple orchard OR spend all day carrying around heavy pumpkins at a pumpkin patch?

Be able to shake cinnamon sugar out of your hair onto your food OR pull apple cinnamon scented stickers off your tongue?

Eat an apple a day for the rest of your life OR find an old apple core in your shoe every day for the rest of your life?

Eat a school cafeteria meal made only from squash OR wear an outfit to school made entirely from dried corn husks?

Would you Rather...

Only be able to play video games after you've raked every single leaf from your yard OR play a video game about being lost in a corn maze?

Get pumpkin pie crust crumbs all over the keyboard of your computer OR mashed potatoes and gravy smeared all over the computer screen?

Would you Rather...

Make all your food into a giant Thanksgiving sandwich OR find out there are no leftovers whatsoever after the meal is over?

Eat a bowl of pumpkin pie flavored breakfast cereal OR eat a bowl of your favorite breakfast cereal with pumpkin pie flavored milk?

Would you Rather...

Eat turkey that is really chewy like beef jerky OR mashed potatoes that are rubbery like a bowl of jello?

Get caught by your friends having your mom take your picture at the pumpkin patch OR have to work cleaning up horse poo at the pumpkin patch's little kid pony ride?

Have the cringy paper turkey you decorated
in kindergarten displayed on your front door
at Thanksgiving OR have your photo taken
wearing a cringy turkey costume on
Thanksgiving Day every year?

Eat a bowl of applesauce that has been mushed
by someone's feet OR an apple pie that is made
from hard and uncooked apples?

Dig potatoes out of your garden with a spoon for Thanksgiving dinner OR comb your hair into a fancy style for the family gathering with a food-crusted fork?

Take your after-dinner-turkey-nap in a treehouse with creaky floorboards OR snuggled up to your dog in his doghouse?

Would you Rather...

Eat a really yummy looking piece of pie that fell into your dirty kitchen sink OR one that fell into the stuffed-full trash can?

Play a game of dodgeball in gym class using rotten apples that have fallen off a tree OR tiny and really hard little acorns that you can throw by the handful?

Drink all the turkey roasting juices out of the pan OR have to finish coloring a turkey placemat before you can eat dinner?

Snuggle up by the warm fire with a cup of hot apple juice that has spicy pepper in it instead of cinnamon OR wearing a cozy pair of slippers with giant holes in the toes that leaves half your feet hanging out?

Be stuck on the sidelines as a cheerleader for the family football game OR be stuck refereeing the game instead of playing?

Pour a ton of thick, brown, gravy on everything you eat for your Thanksgiving meal OR drink a big ole' glass of brown gravy after stuffing your face on Thanksgiving?

Roll around in a pile of hay wearing only your swimsuit OR dive into a giant dirty pit of dried up corn kernels?

Have a giant blowup turkey in the corner of your bedroom the week before Thanksgiving OR wear a giant blowup turkey costume to school on the day before Thanksgiving?

Wear a crown made out of fallen pinecones that poke into your head OR wear a hat made out of a hollowed out pumpkin shell that is still goopy inside?

Dig into a plateful of yams that turn out to be earwax OR get passed your favorite dish of food right after your grandpa coughs all over it?

Chill out in front of the TV with a blanket and a moldy leaf scented candle OR have to watch an hour long show on how to properly peel apples?

Have to find your way through a corn maze to get to the playground for recess OR have your school cafeteria magically transported outside to picnic tables?

Grow two very large front teeth like a squirrel and begin gnawing all of your food OR become nocturnal like an owl and swoop down out of trees hunting mice at night?

Dress up like one of the original Pilgrims for Thanksgiving OR eat your meal using only the utensils available to the first Pilgrims - spoons and knives, no forks?

Have a big black crow follow you wherever you go like a pet OR have a squirrel decide to make its home in your backpack?

Eat deer or seafood for Thanksgiving like the first Pilgrims probably did OR live in a log cabin that has no flushing toilets and only a fireplace for heat?

Be a beautiful orange pumpkin covered with green warty looking bumps OR an almost perfectly round orange pumpkin with a really big dent in it at the pumpkin patch?

Go to a school that has outhouses for bathrooms OR a school that doesn't have pencil sharpeners?

Would you Rather...

Find a bunch of crunched up leaves in your underwear OR have a big clump of dried mud fall out of your belly button?

Have to sit at the kiddie table with a bunch of toddlers for dinner OR get to sit at the adult table surrounded by your partly deaf grandparents who can't hear what you say and yell everything they say?

Get bounced off a hayride into a big squishy mud puddle OR step on a smelly rotten pumpkin at the pumpkin patch?

Eat soup for every meal in the months of September and October OR eat a lettuce salad with cranberries and walnuts every day during September and October?

Have crunchy green corn husks on your head instead of hair OR drool melted caramel whenever you smell food?

Have to wear a bunch of stretched out hand-me-down sweaters from your cousin OR have to take a super cheesy family photo where everyone wears a matching outfit and while you are taking the photo a bunch of your frenemies see you?

Would you Rather...

Drink a big cup of steaming hot chocolate out of a pumpkin shell OR eat a steaming pile of cooked pumpkin drizzled with fudge sauce?

Spend your Friday night at a really boring football game that has no score after two hours OR a really exciting football game, but mosquitos are eating you alive?

Would you Rather...

Play a game of soccer with your friends using a pumpkin OR play Marco Polo in a pool of apple juice?

Live in a warm place where the leaves stay green all year OR live in a cool place where the leaves change to beautiful shades of red, orange, and gold?

98

Eat one meatloaf per day every day for a month OR sleep on top of a giant meatloaf for a week straight?

Bake the apple pie and forget to add sugar to it so there are just really sour apples baked into a crust OR accidentally leave the vanilla ice cream on the counter so it is poured on top of your pie like gravy?

Eat a piece of pumpkin pie out of your sneaker OR eat a piece of apple pie out of a dirty baseball cap?

Hide in a corn maze and scare kids walking by Or get scared so bad by a kid hiding in the maze that you wet your pants?

Get hit in the face by an apple pie OR have a giant container of applesauce dumped over your head?

Eat Thanksgiving dinner on a table that is really sticky so everything that touches it sticks to the table OR on a table that is really slippery so the dishes and silverware keep sliding right off of the table?

Have the bushy tail of a squirrel that is always knocking things over OR the painted-on face of a scarecrow that only shows one emotion?

Sail across the ocean on the Mayflower for 66 days like the Pilgrims OR eat a full Thanksgiving meal once a day for 66 days straight?

Would You Rather...

Sleep overnight in a cave next to a warm fuzzy hibernating bear OR come across a wide-awake bear while hiking in the woods?

Build a miniature log cabin using your green bean casserole OR try to construct a perfect teepee by flattening your dinner roll and using your fork and spoon?

Would you Rather...

Eat a bowl of pumpkin soup that tastes like liquid earwax OR eat a bowl of beet stew that tastes like dirt?

Tailgate at your favorite team's football game when it is only twenty degrees outside, and you're wrapped in a blanket shivering OR tailgate in the hot baking sun on an eighty-five-degree day?

Swim ten laps across an Olympic-sized pool of apple cinnamon oatmeal OR run five laps around a track that has a layer of slimy applesauce all over it?

Wear a shirt made entirely from super sweet orange, yellow, and white candy corns OR made from faded, wrinkled, old Halloween candy wrappers?

Have a two-hour long conversation with a brainless scarecrow OR the nerdiest person you know?

Find ants crawling all over the stick that you are roasting your marshmallow on OR find ants crawling up the arm that you are holding your marshmallow stick with?

Have a tree climbing contest with a squirrel OR a hole digging contest with your dog?

Work as the person who helps people find their way out of a corn maze OR as the person who drives a hayride, doing the same circle over and over?

Did you enjoy the book?

If you did, we are ecstatic. If not, please write your complaint to us, and we will make sure to fix it.

If you're feeling generous, there is something important that you can help me with – tell other people that you enjoyed the book.

Ask a grown-up to write about it on Amazon. When they do, more people will find out about the book. It also lets Amazon know that we are making kids around the world laugh. Even a few words and ratings would go a long way.

If you have any ideas or jokes that you think are super funny, please let us know. We would love to hear from you. Our email address is - **riddleland@riddlelandforkids.com**

Bonus Book!

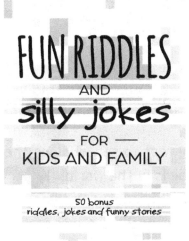

FUN RIDDLES
AND
silly jokes
— FOR —
KIDS AND FAMILY

50 bonus
riddles, jokes and funny stories

RIDDLELAND

https://pixelfy.me/riddlelandbonus

Thank you for buying this book. We would like to share a special bonus as a token of appreciation. It is a collection of 50 original jokes, riddles, and two super funny stories!

109

Would you like your jokes and riddles to be featured in our next book?

We are having a contest to see who are the smartest or funniest boys and girls in the world! :

1) Creative and Challenging Riddles

2) Tickle Your Funny Bone Contest

Parents, please email us your child's "Original" Riddle or Joke and **he or she could win a $50 Amazon gift card and be featured in our next book.**

Here are the rules:

1) It must be challenging for the riddles and funny for the jokes!

2) It must be 100% original and not something from the Internet! It is easy to find out!

3) You can submit both jokes and riddles as they are 2 separate contests.

4) No help from the parents unless they are as funny as you.

5) Winners will be announced via email or our Facebook group

   – Riddleland for kids

6) Please also mention what book you purchased.

7) Email us at Riddleland@riddlelandforkids.com

Other Fun Children Books for The Kids!

Riddles Series

Try Not to Laugh Challenge Series

Would You Rather... Series

Get them on Amazon
or our website at www.riddlelandforkids.com

About Riddleland

Riddleland is a mom + dad run publishing company. We are passionate about creating fun and innovative books to help children develop their reading skills and fall in love with reading. If you have suggestions for us or want to work with us, shoot us an email at riddleland@riddlelandforkids.com

Our favourite family quote

"Creativity is an area in which younger people have a tremendous advantage since they have an endearing habit of always questioning past wisdom and authority." – Bill Hewlett

Made in the USA
Las Vegas, NV
22 November 2020